Boy

W9-CPA-602

| 1 | 2 |
| 3 | 4 |

Skill: Cut and paste in order.

Girl

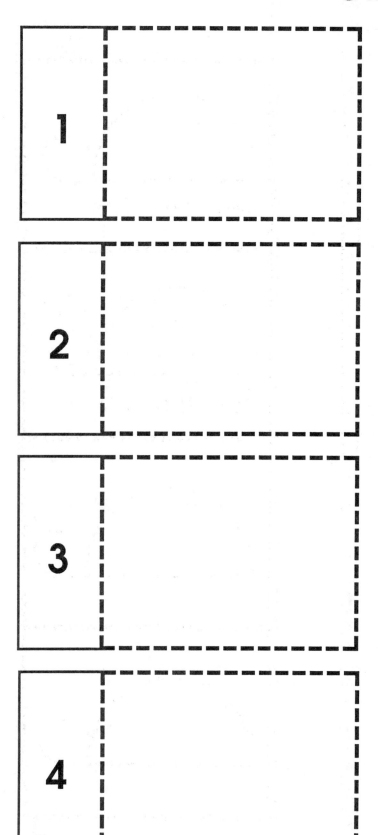

2

FS-32026 Critical Thinking

Ladybug

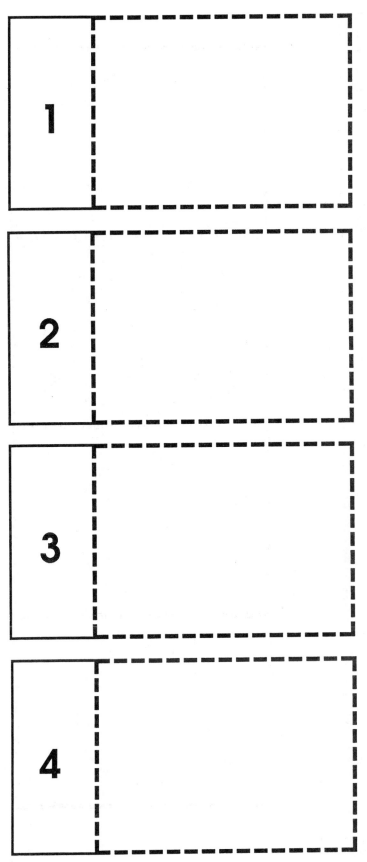

3

Worm

1

2

3

4

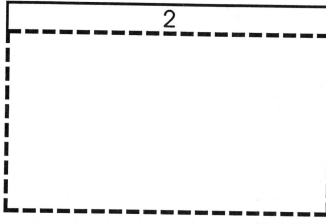
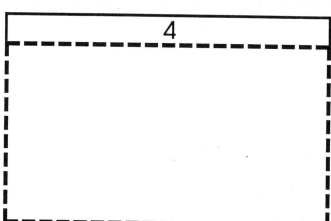
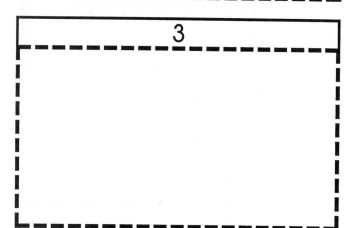

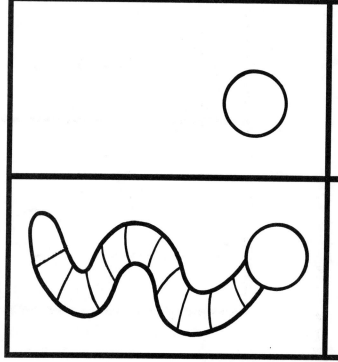

FS-32026 Critical Thinking

Butterfly

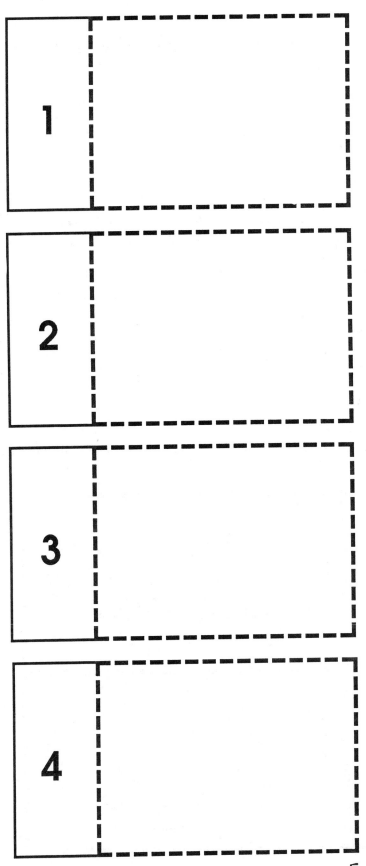

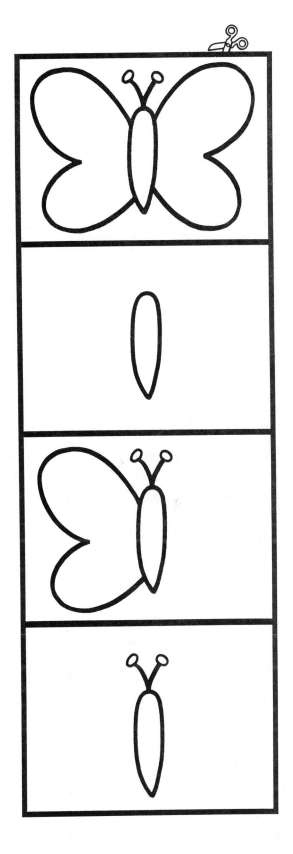

Bunny

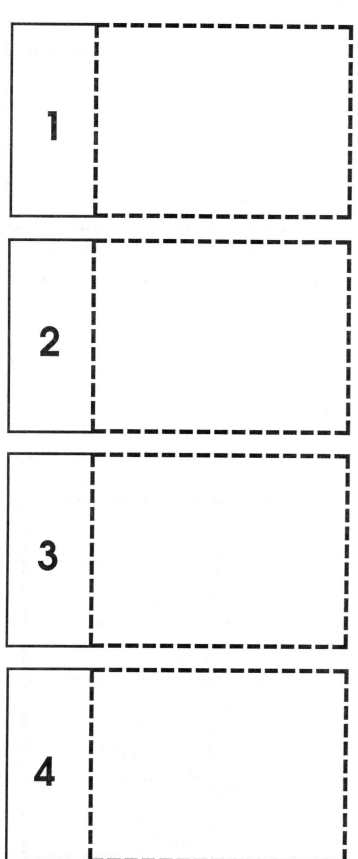

6

FS-32026 Critical Thinking

Teddy Bear

1	2

3	4

FS-32026 Critical Thinking

Snowman

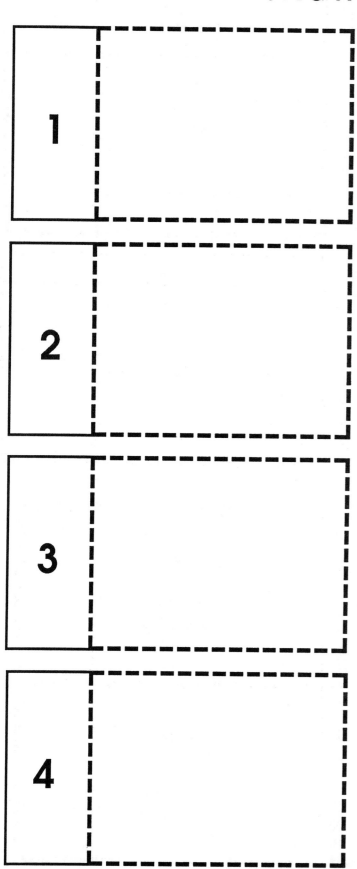

8

Sun

1	2
3	4

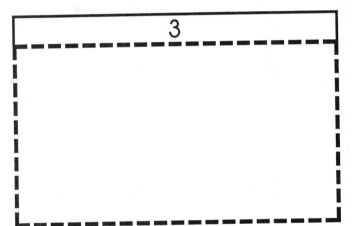
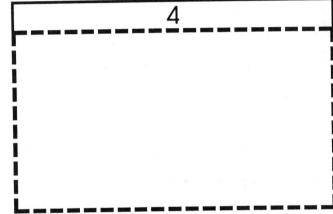

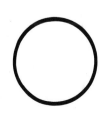

9

FS-32026 Critical Thinking

House

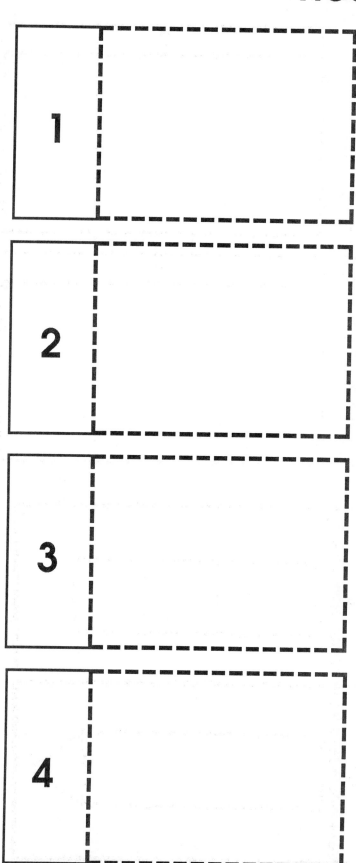

10

Pencil

1	2

3	4

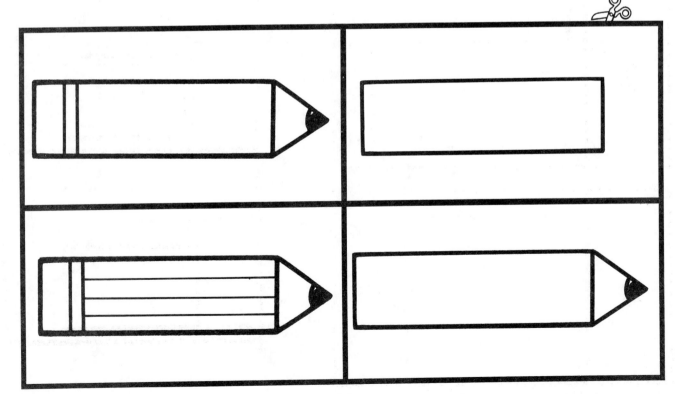

FS-32026 Critical Thinking

Name _____

School Bus

1	2
3	4

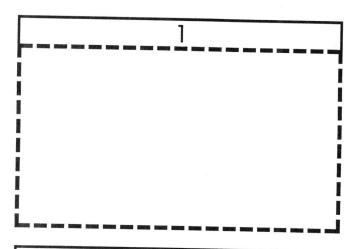
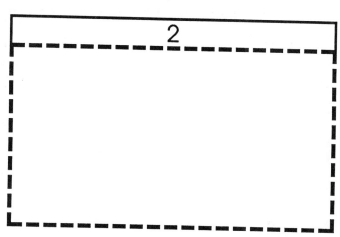
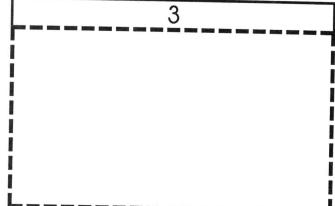
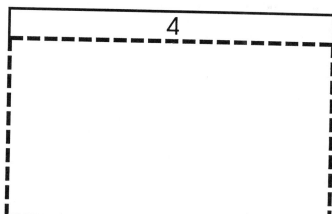

School Bus

12

FS-32026 Critical Thinking

Umbrella

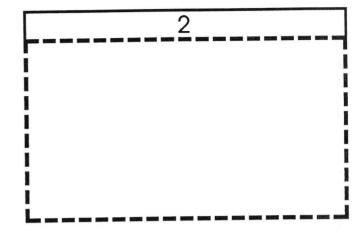

1

2

3

4

FS-32026 Critical Thinking

Balloons

1	2

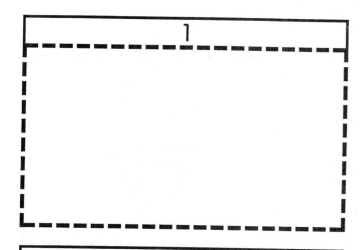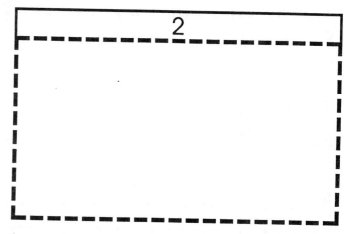

3	4

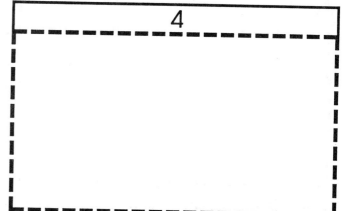

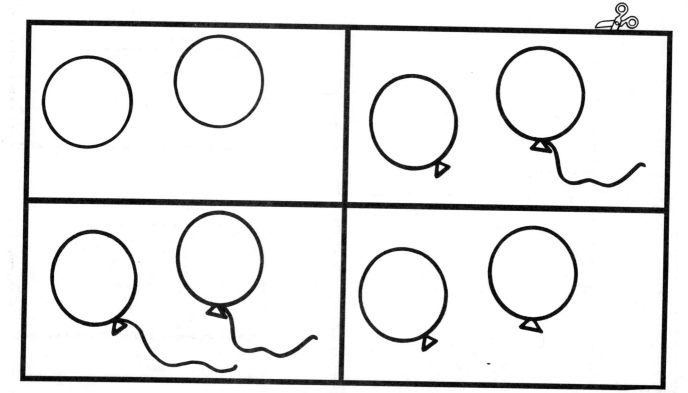

Ice Cream Cone

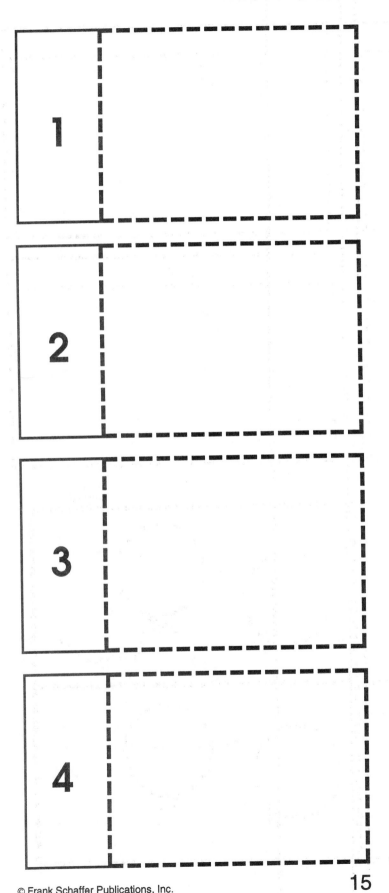

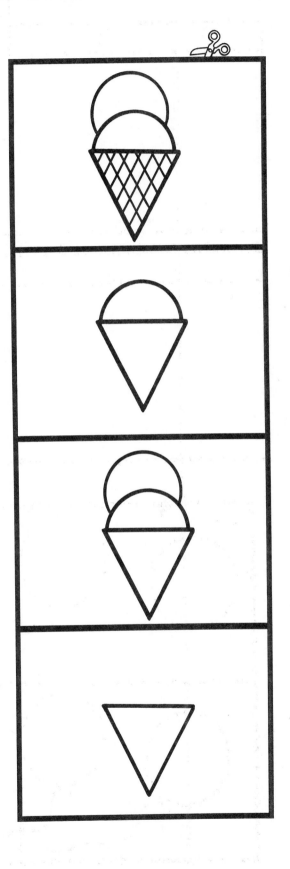

15

FS-32026 Critical Thinking

Name _____

Fruit Bowl

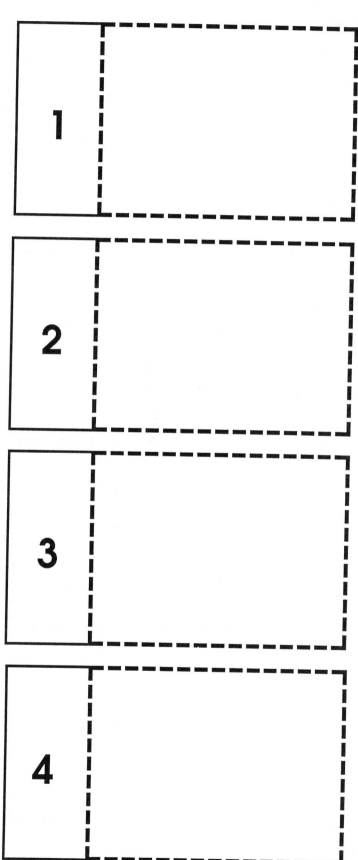

16

FS-32026 Critical Thinking

Name _____

Flower

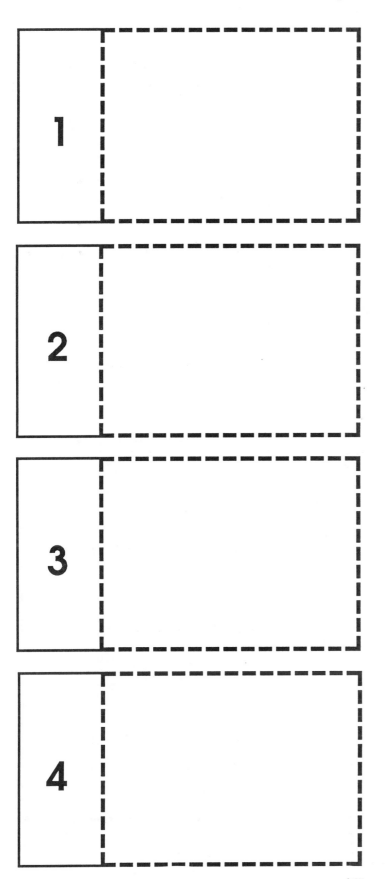

17

FS-32026 Critical Thinking

Robot

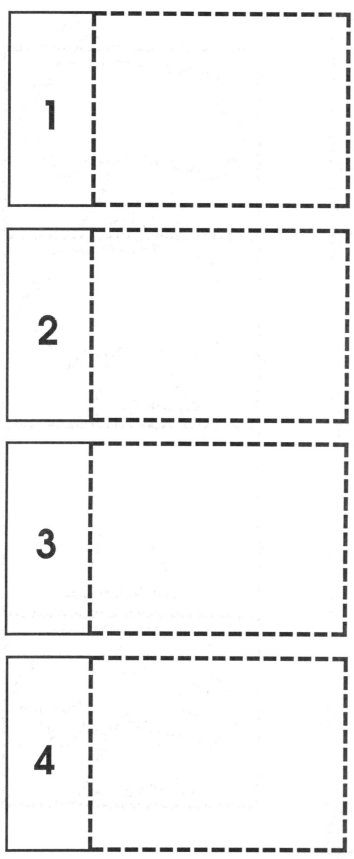

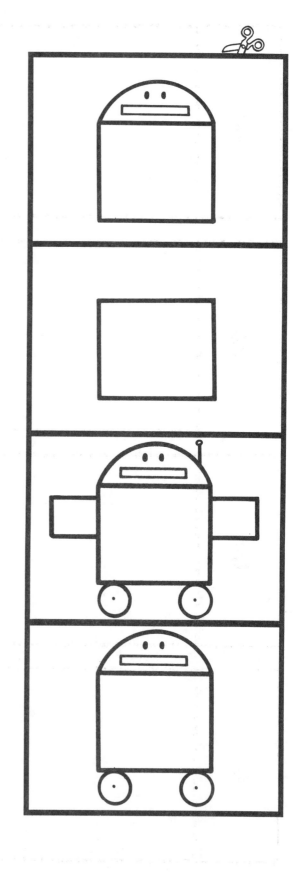

Apple Tree

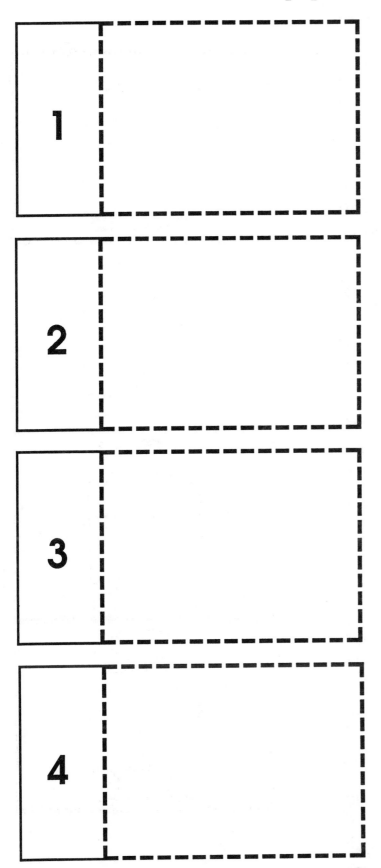

Skill: Cut and paste in order.

Getting Dressed

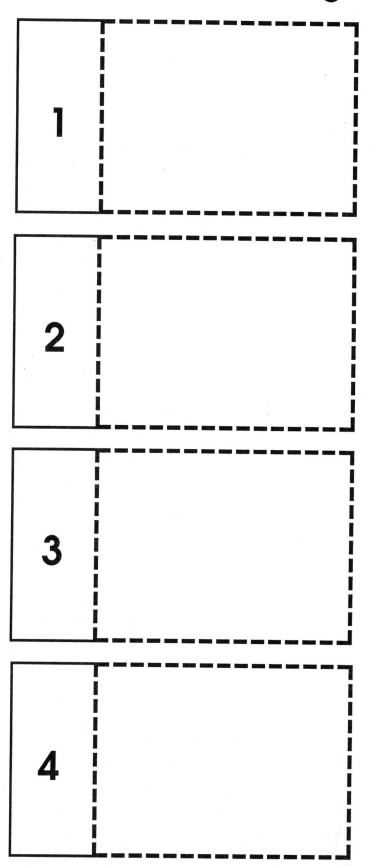

FS-32026 Critical Thinking

Name _____

1	**2**
3	**4**

Cut out the pictures. Paste them in order above.

Name _____

1	**2**
3	**4**

Cut out the pictures. Paste them in order above.

Name _____

1	**2**
3	**4**

Cut out the pictures. Paste them in order above.

1	**2**
3	**4**

Cut out the pictures. Paste them in order above.

1	**2**
3	**4**

Cut out the pictures. Paste them in order above.

1	**2**
3	**4**

Cut out the pictures. Paste them in order above.

Name _____

1	**2**
3	**4**

Cut out the pictures. Paste them in order above.

FS-32026 Critical Thinking

Name _____

1	**2**
3	**4**

Cut out the pictures. Paste them in order above.

1	**2**
3	**4**

Cut out the pictures. Paste them in order above.

FS-32026 Critical Thinking

Name _____

1	**2**
3	**4**

Cut out the pictures. Paste them in order above.

1	**2**
3	**4**

Cut out the pictures. Paste them in order above.

Name _____

1	**2**
3	**4**

Cut out the pictures. Paste them in order above.

1	**2**
3	**4**

Cut out the pictures. Paste them in order above.

Name _____

1	**2**
3	**4**

Cut out the pictures. Paste them in order above.

1	**2**
3	**4**

Cut out the pictures. Paste them in order above.

Name _____   Draw a line between the matching cats. Then color the kitties.

Name _____

Draw a line to each twin.
Color all the turtles.

37

FS-32026 Critical Thinking

Name _____

Circle all the cats that are exactly the same. Color the page in your favorite colors.

Name _____

Circle all of the snakes that are the same. Then color the snakes in your favorite colors.

FS-32026 Critical Thinking

Name _____

Circle the twins in each row.
Color all the pictures.

FS-32026 Critical Thinking

Name _____

Follow the pattern.
Finish each row.

© Frank Schaffer Publications, Inc.

FS-32026 Critical Thinking

Follow the pattern.
Finish each row.

a b a b a b

c d d c d d

e e a e e a

m n m n m n

o e o e o e

d d e d d e

a b c a b c

a m a m a m

Name _____ Draw the missing half,
then color the picture.

43

Name _____

Draw the missing half.
Color the picture.

Name _____   Draw the missing half.
Color the picture.

FS-32026 Critical Thinking

Name _____

Put an X on each hidden heart.
(There are at least 20.)
Then color the picture.

46

How Do They Feel?

Circle the face that shows how you would feel.
Color the pictures.

Name ______________________________

Skill: Making inferences – Determining feelings

How Do They Feel?

Circle the face that shows how you would feel.
Color the pictures.

1.

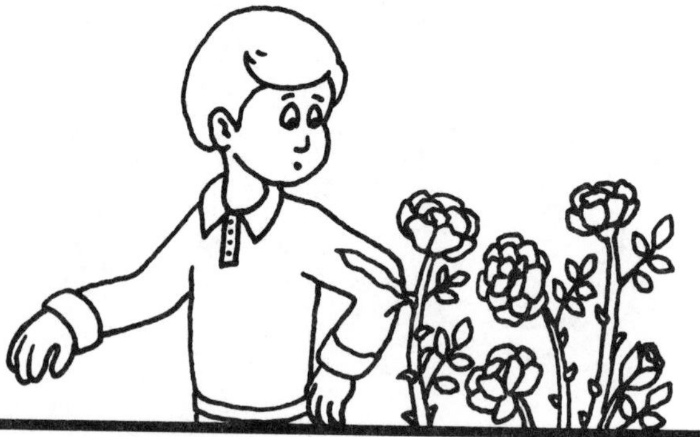

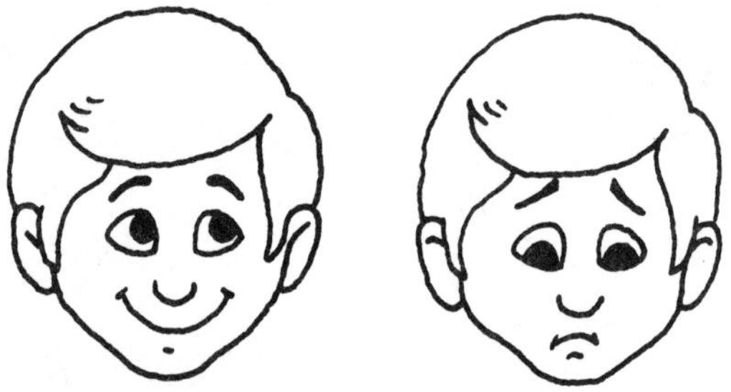

2.

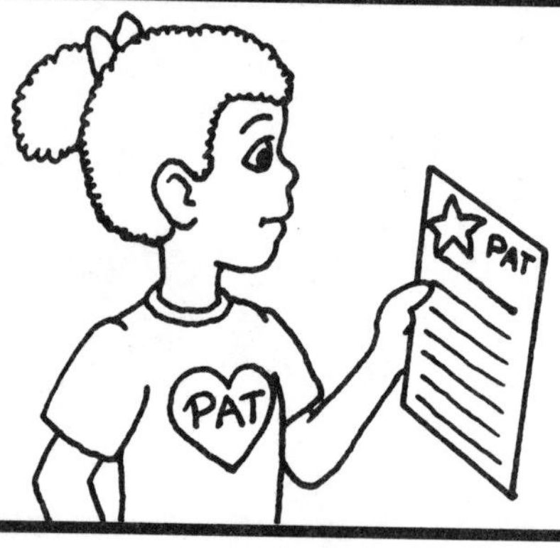

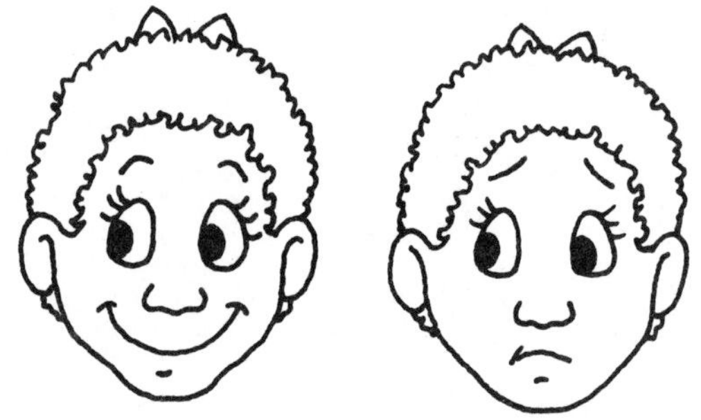

3.

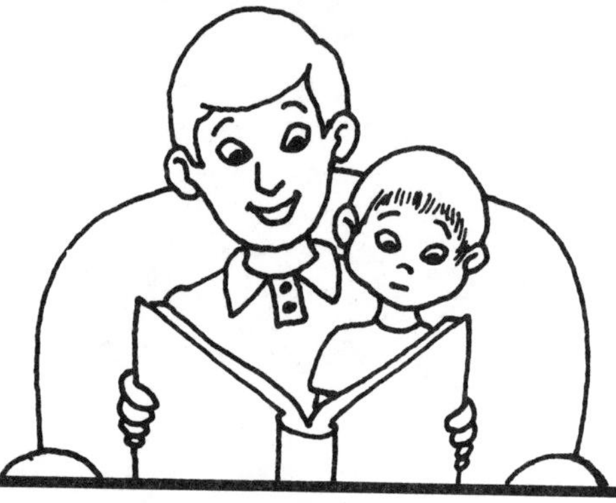

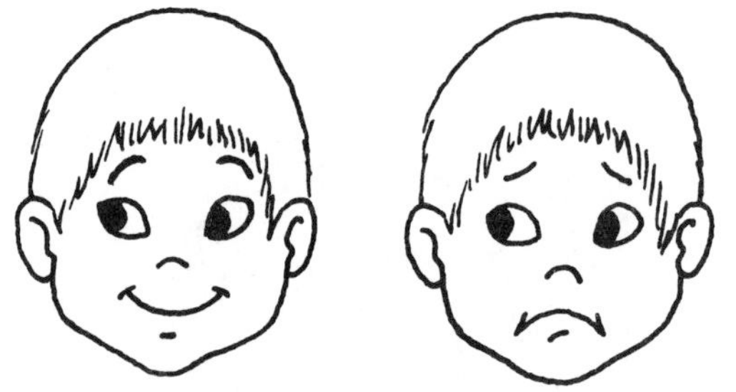

4.

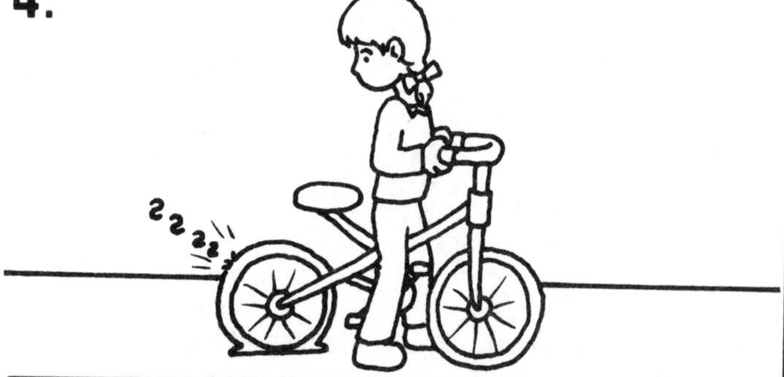

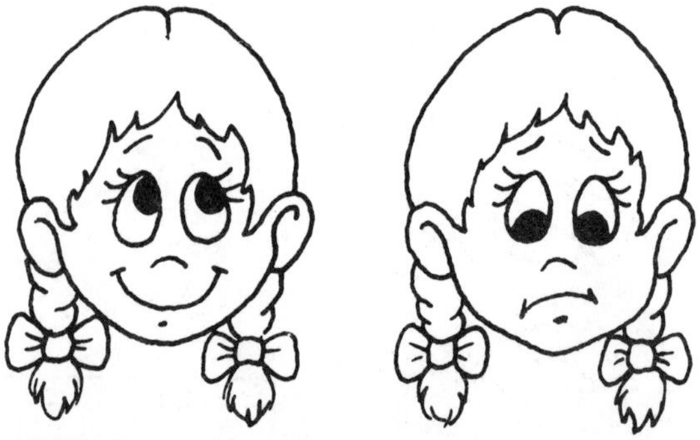

Can It Happen?

In each row, color the picture that shows what **cannot** really happen.

1.

2.

3.

4.

FS-32026 Critical Thinking

Who Needs This?

Look at the first picture in each row.
Color the picture that shows who needs it.

Who Needs This?

Look at the first picture in each row.
Color the picture that shows who needs it.

1.

2.

3.

4.

Who Lives Here?

Look at the home in each row.
Color the animal that lives there.

Where Are They?

Color the picture that shows where each person is.

FS-32026 Critical Thinking

What Do They See?

Circle the picture that shows what each one sees.
Color the pictures.

Time to Pack

Look at the first picture in each row.
Circle the two things you can put in it.

1.

Munch your Lunch!

2.

Greta's Market

MILK

3.

4.

What Can You Make?

Cut and paste to show what you can make.

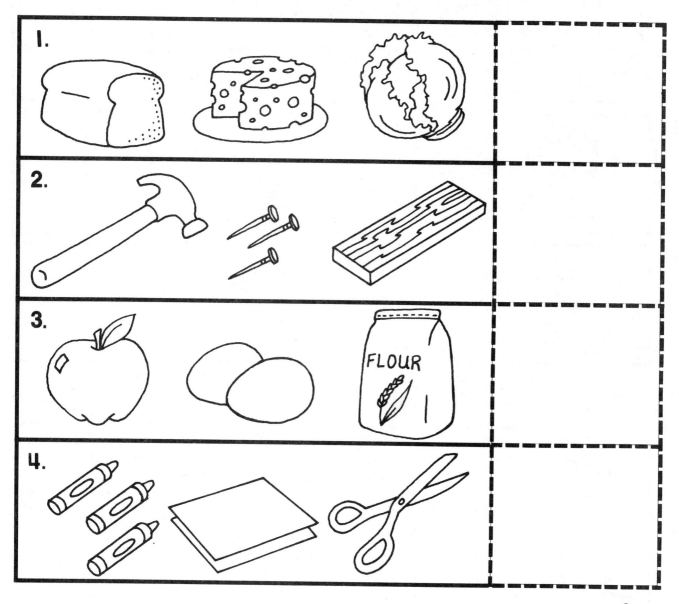

Name _____

What Comes Next?

Cut out the boxes at the bottom of the page. Paste them in the right places.

Name _____

What Comes Next?

Cut out the boxes at the bottom of the page. Paste them in the right places.

1.

2.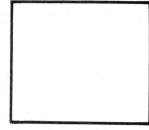

3.

4.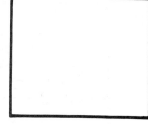

5.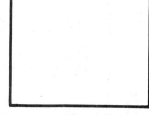

 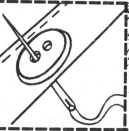  

58

FS-32026 Critical Thinking

Name _____

What Comes Next?

Cut out the boxes at the bottom of the page. Paste them in the right places.

1.

2.

3.

4.

5.

What Happens Next?

Cut out the boxes at the bottom of the page.
Paste them in the right places.

What Happens Next?

Cut out the boxes at the bottom of the page.
Paste them in the right places.

Name _____

Finish the Pattern

Cut out the pictures at the bottom of the page.
Paste them in the right places.

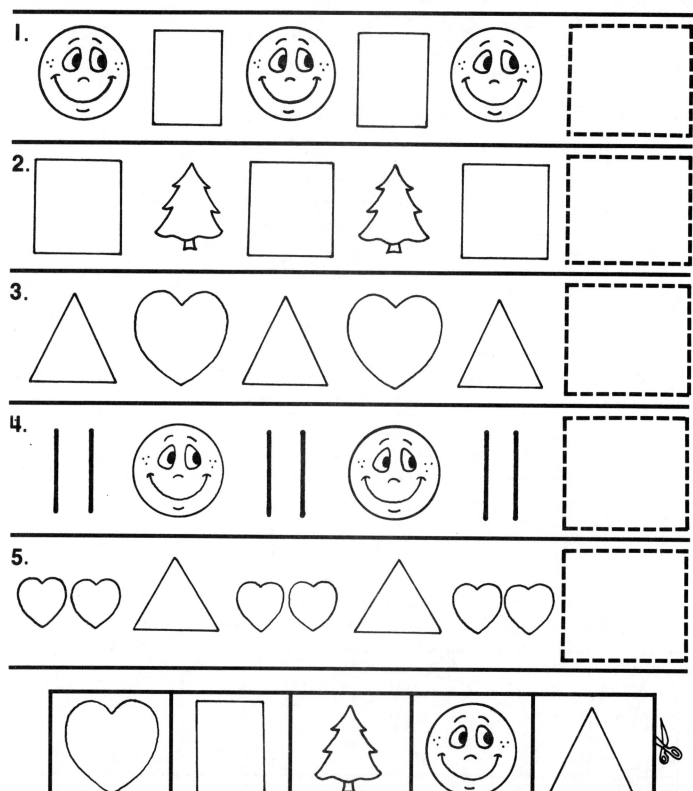

Where Are They Going?

Draw a line to show where each child is going.
Color the pictures.

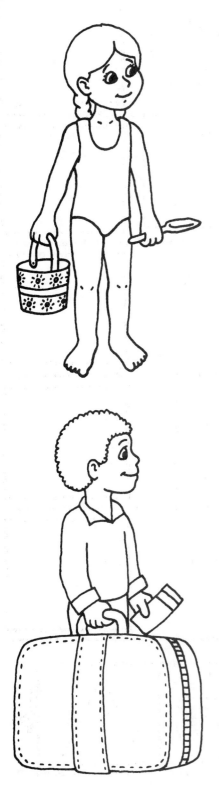

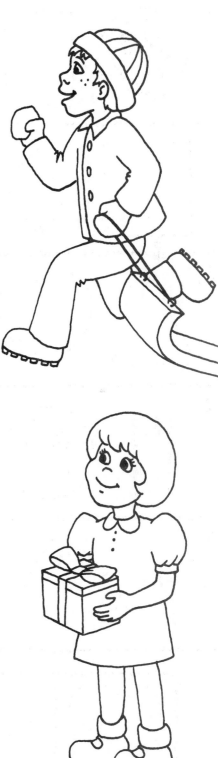

63

FS-32026 Critical Thinking

Where Are They Going?

Draw a line to show where each person is going.
Color the pictures.

64

FS-32026 Critical Thinking

Where Does It Belong?

Draw a line to show where each thing belongs.
Color the pictures.

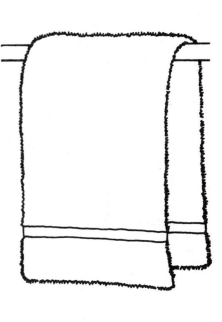

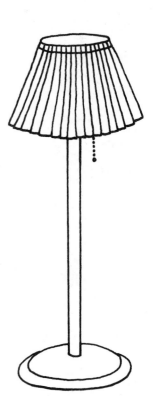

65

FS-32026 Critical Thinking

What Do They Need?

Draw a line to show what each person needs.
Color the pictures.

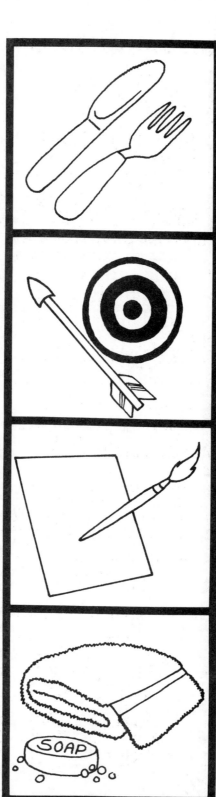

Wash Time

Draw a line to show what each person is going to wash.
Color the pictures.

Find the Mistakes

Circle the part in each picture that does not belong.
Color all the pictures.

FS-32026 Critical Thinking

Skill: Making inferences

Find the Mistakes

Circle the part in each picture that does not belong.
Color all the pictures.

FS-32026 Critical Thinking

Name _____

Circle the mistakes.
(There are at least 15.)
Then color the picture.

Name _____

Circle the mistakes.
(There are at least 15.)
Then color all the pictures.

71

Name _____

Circle the mistakes in this picture.
(There are at least 22.)
Color the picture.

72

1.

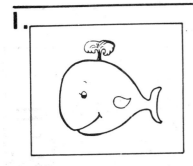  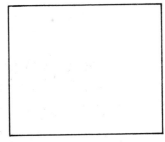

2.

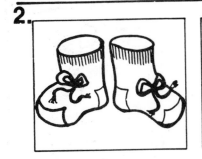 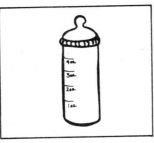  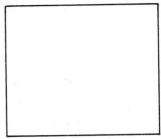

3.

   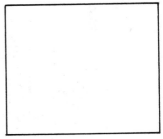

4.

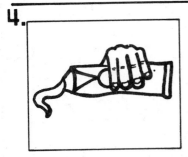   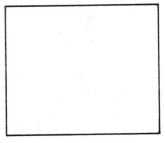

Cut out the pictures below. Match each picture with the right group. Paste it in the square.

 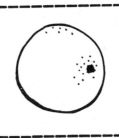  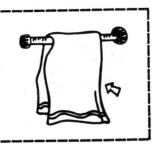

73

1.

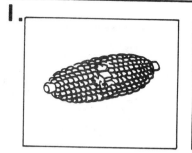  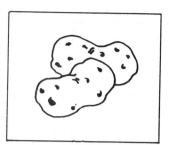 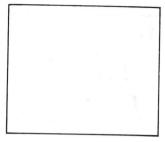

2.

   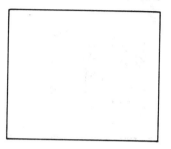

3.

   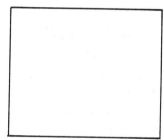

4.

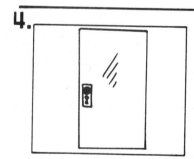   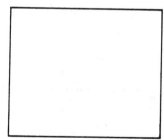

Cut out the pictures below. Match each picture with the right group. Paste it in the square.

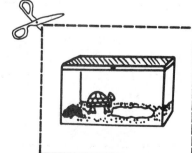   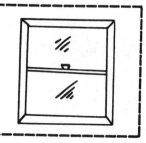

FS-32026 Critical Thinking

Name _____ Skill: Categorization

Circle three things in each row that go together.

1.

2.

3.

4.

5.

6.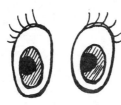

FS-32026 Critical Thinking

Name _____

Circle the thing that does not belong in each box. Draw a line to show where it should be.

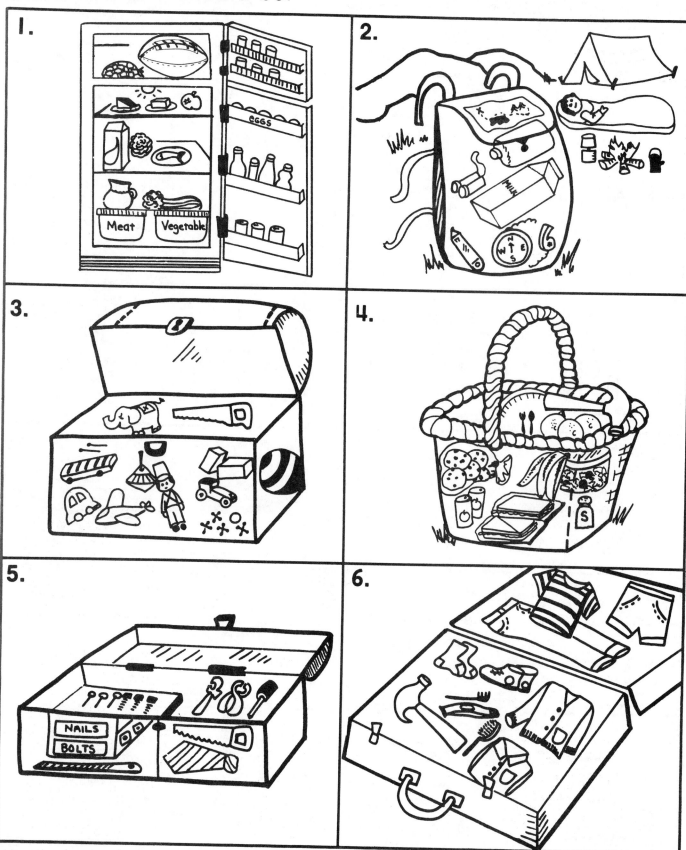

1.	2.	3.

Cut out the pictures below. Paste them under the right pictures.

FS-32026 Critical Thinking

Cut out the pictures below. Paste them under the right pictures.

Name _____

Color things you find . . .

. . . inside the house ▸ red

. . . outside the house ▸ green

Name _____

Color things that go . . .

. . . on water 〰〰 [yellow]

. . . on land 〰 [red]

. . . in the sky ☁☁ [blue]

80

1.
2.
3.

4.
5.
6.

Cut out the pictures below. Paste each sports item under the person who uses it.

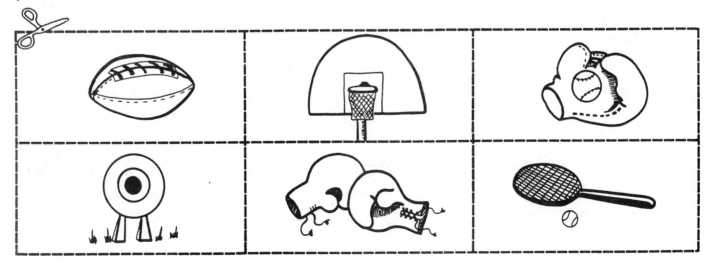

FS-32026 Critical Thinking

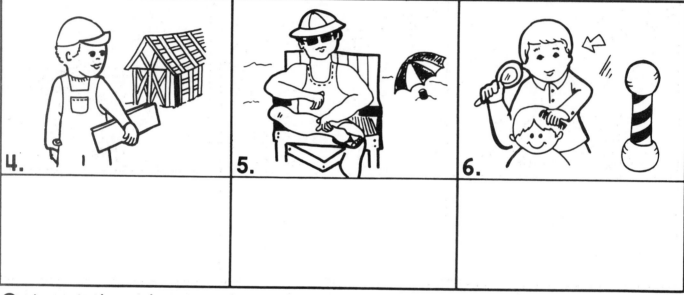

Cut out the pictures below. Paste each item under the person who uses it.

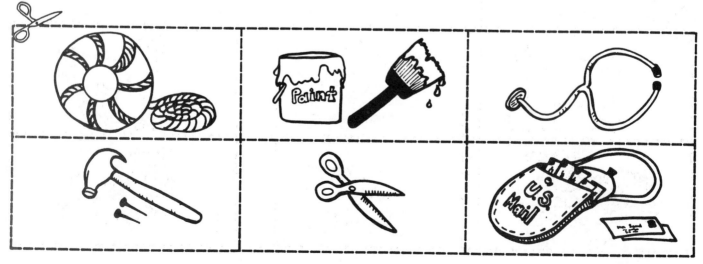

Cut out the baby animals below. Paste each baby under its mother.

FS-32026 Critical Thinking

1.

2.

Cut out the pictures below. Paste them in the right places.

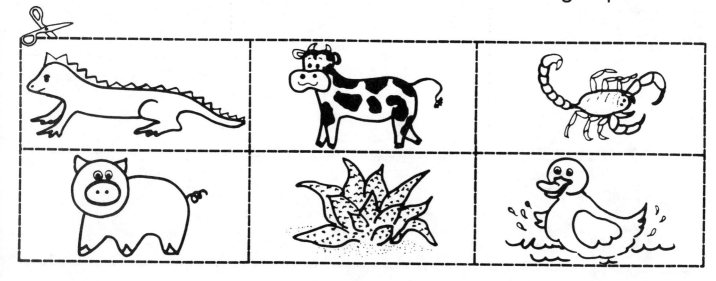

1.
2.
3.
4.

Cut and paste the pictures below to make each pair go together in the same way.

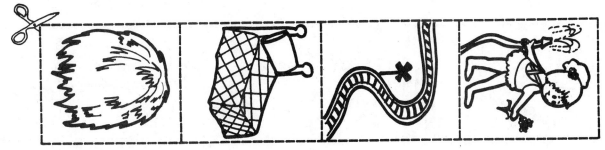

1.

2.

3.

4.

Cut and paste the pictures below to make each pair go together in the same way.

86

FS-32026 Critical Thinking

1.

2.

3.

4.

Cut and paste the pictures below to make each pair go together in the same way.

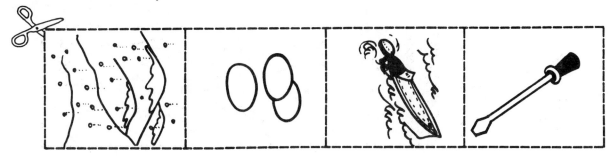

87

Find the Causes

Cut and paste the cause to match the effect.

Cause	Effect	Cause

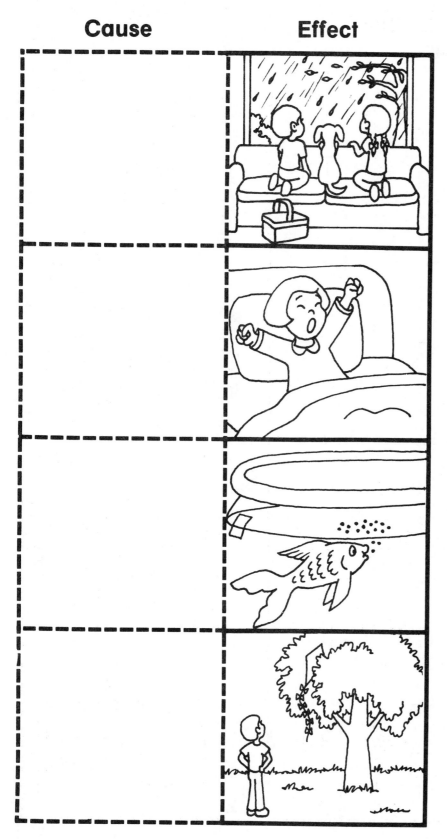

FS-32026 Critical Thinking

Find the Causes

Cut and paste the cause to match the effect.

Cause   **Effect**   **Cause**

Find the Causes

Cut and paste the cause to match the effect.

Cause   **Effect**   **Cause**

FS-32026 Critical Thinking

Find the Causes

Cut and paste the cause to match the effect.

Cause	Effect	Cause

FS-32026 Critical Thinking

Find the Effects

Cut and paste the effect to match the cause.

Cause　　　　　**Effect**　　　　　**Effect** ✂

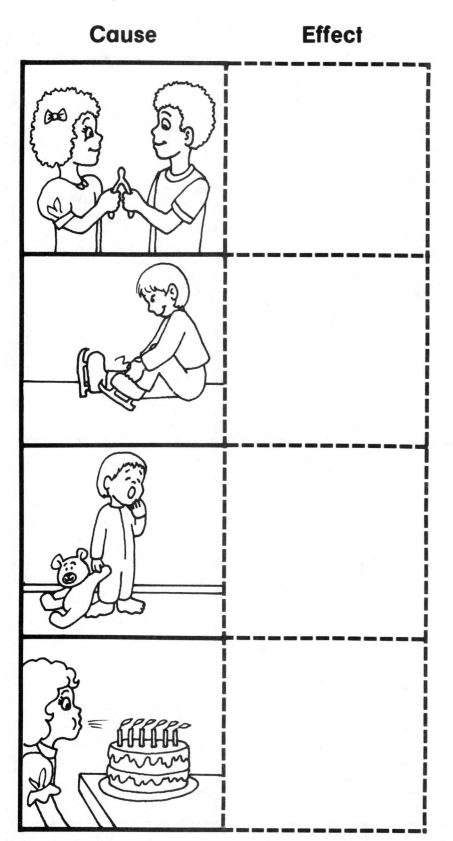

FS-32026 Critical Thinking

Find the Effects

Cut and paste the effect to match the cause.

Cause   **Effect**   **Effect**

Find the Effects

Cut and paste the effect to match the cause.

Cause   **Effect**   **Effect** ✂

Find the Effects

Cut and paste the effect to match the cause.

FS-32026 Critical Thinking

Make Three Nursery Rhyme Puzzles

Cut and match the cause and effect puzzle pieces.

Example:

Matching Cause and Effect

Cause   **Effect**

FS-32026 Critical Thinking

Matching Cause and Effect

Cause   **Effect**

FS-32026 Critical Thinking

Matching Cause and Effect

Cause

Effect

FS-32026 Critical Thinking

Matching Cause and Effect

Cause   **Effect**

FS-32026 Critical Thinking

What Happened to Make the Flower Grow?

Color the causes of the flower growing.

Name _____

What Happened to Make the Rainbow Appear?

Color the causes of the rainbow appearing.

What Happens When It Rains?

Color the effects of rain.

103

What Happens When You Move?

Color the effects of moving.

Answer Key

Name _____ Skill: Cut and paste in order.

Girl

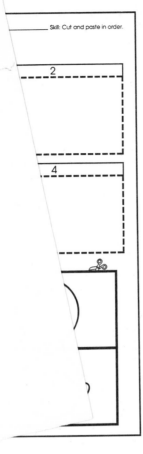

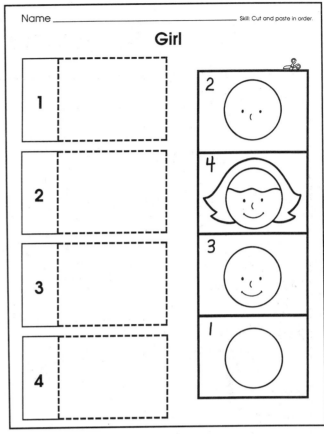

Page 2

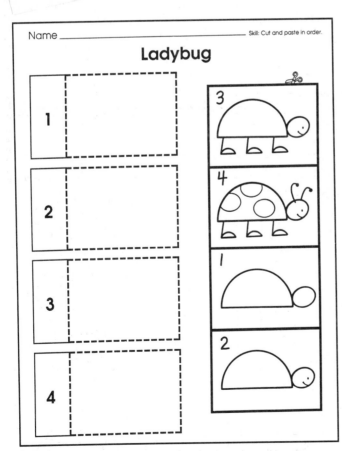

Name _____ Skill: Cut and paste in order.

Ladybug

1	
2	
3	
4	

Page 3

Name _____ Skill: Cut and paste in order.

Worm

Page 4

Answer Key

Butterfly

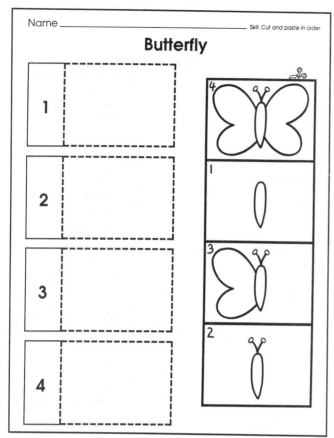

Page 5

Bunny

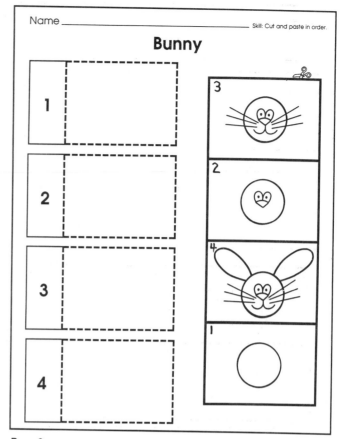

Page 6

Teddy Bear

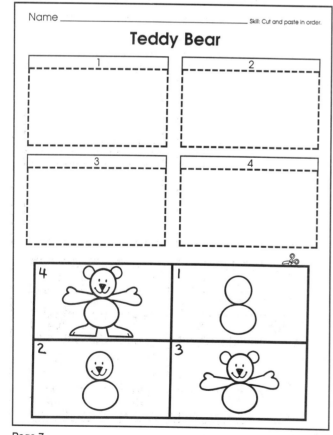

Page 7

Snowman

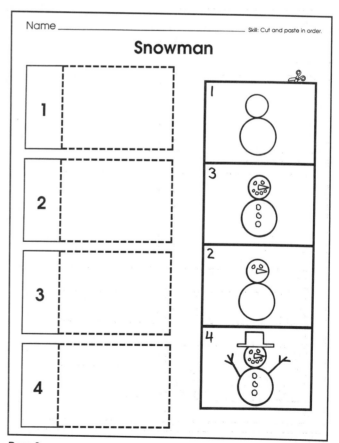

Page 8

Answer Key

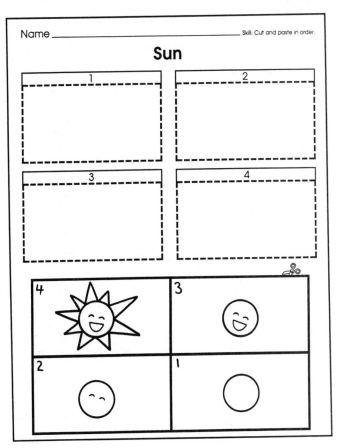

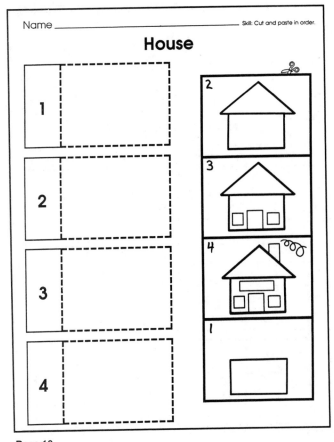

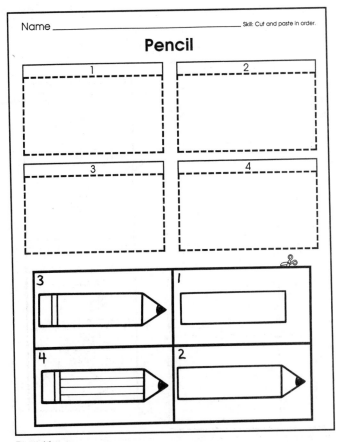

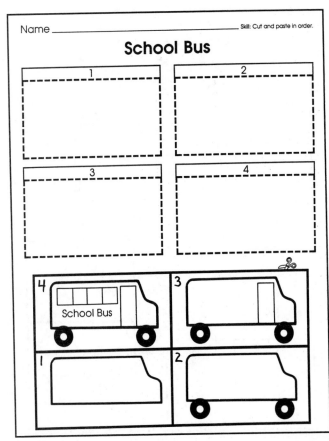

FS-32026 Critical Thinking

Answer Key

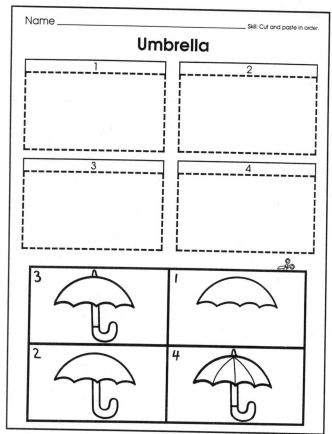

Page 13

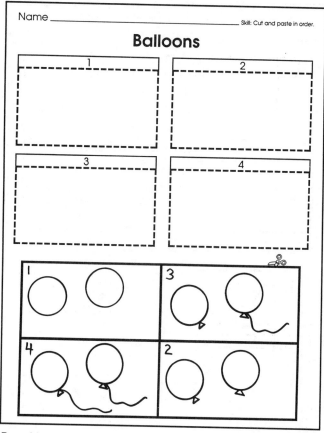

Page 14

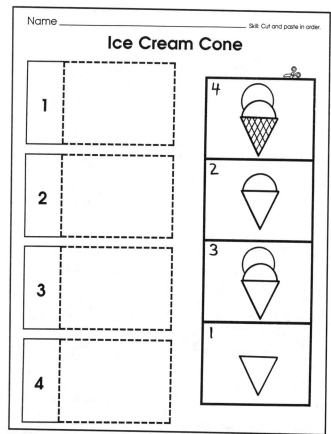

Page 15

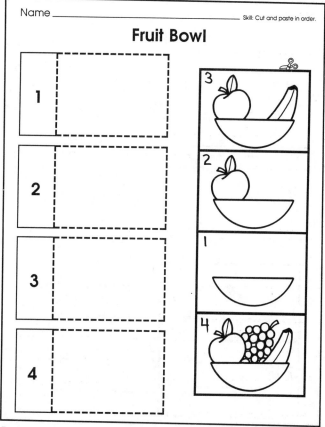

Page 16

108

Answer Key

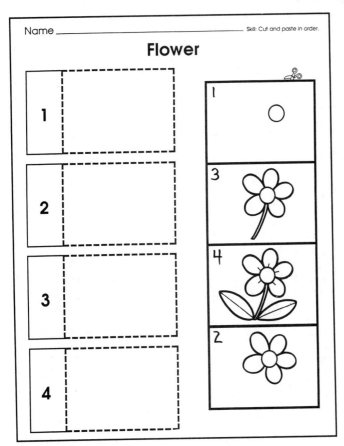

Page 17

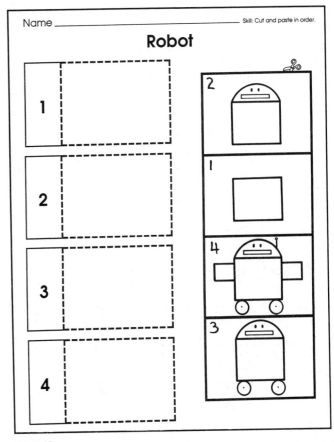

Page 18

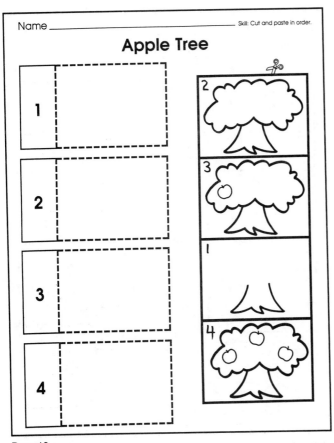

Page 19

Page 20

109

Answer Key

Name _____

1	2
3	4

Cut out the pictures. Paste them in order above.

Page 21

Name _____

1	2
3	4

Cut out the pictures. Paste them in order above.

Page 22

Name _____

1	2
3	4

Cut out the pictures. Paste them in order above.

Page 23

Name _____

1	2
3	4

Cut out the pictures. Paste them in order above.

Page 24

FS-32026 Critical Thinking

Answer Key

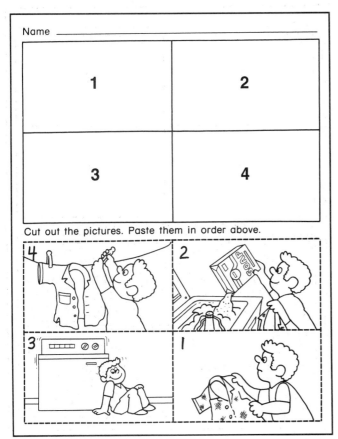

Cut out the pictures. Paste them in order above.

Page 25

Cut out the pictures. Paste them in order above.

Page 26

Cut out the pictures. Paste them in order above.

Page 27

Cut out the pictures. Paste them in order above.

Page 28

FS-32026 Critical Thinking

Answer Key

Page 29

Page 30

Page 31

Page 32

112

Answer Key

Name

Page 33

Page 34

Page 35

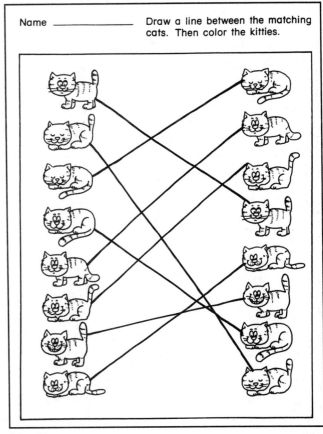

Page 36

113

Answer Key

Name _____ Draw a line to each twin. Color all the turtles.

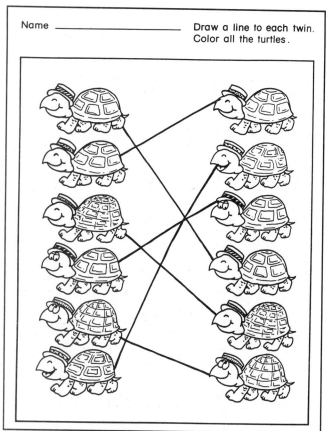

Name _____ Circle all the cats that are exactly the same. Color the page in your favorite colors.

Name _____ Circle all of the snakes that are the same. Then color the snakes in your favorite colors.

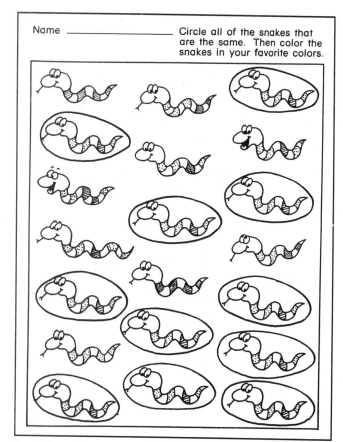

Name _____ Circle the twins in each row. Color all the pictures.

FS-32026 Critical Thinking

Answer Key

Name _____ Follow the pattern. Finish each row.

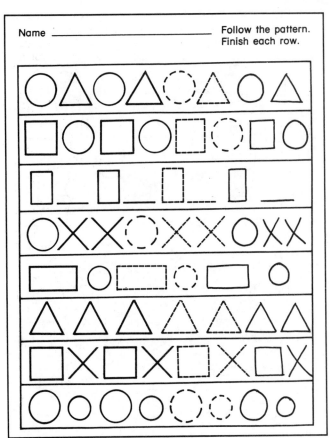

Page 41

Name _____ Follow the pattern. Finish each row.

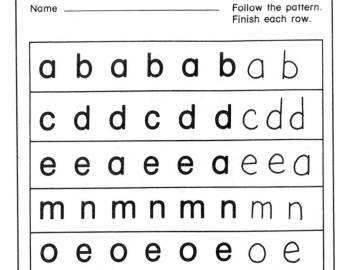

Page 42

Name _____ Draw the missing half, then color the picture.

Page 43

Name _____ Draw the missing half. Color the picture.

Page 44

115

FS-32026 Critical Thinking

Answer Key

Name _____ Draw the missing half.
Color the picture.

Page 45

Name _____ Put an X on each hidden heart.
(There are at least 20.)
Then color the picture.

Page 46

Name _____ Skill: Making inferences –
Determining feelings

How Do They Feel?

Circle the face that shows how you would feel.
Color the pictures.

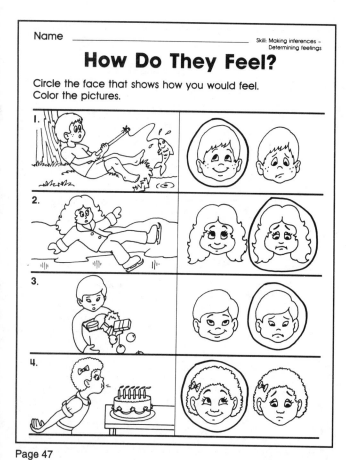

Page 47

Name _____ Skill: Making inferences –
Determining feelings

How Do They Feel?

Circle the face that shows how you would feel.
Color the pictures.

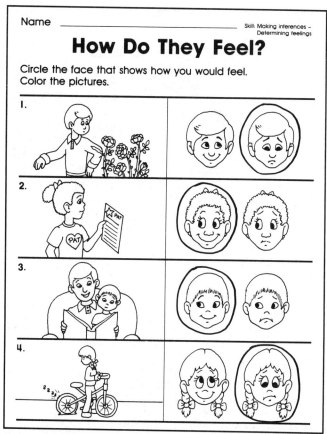

Page 48

116

FS-32026 Critical Thinking

Answer Key

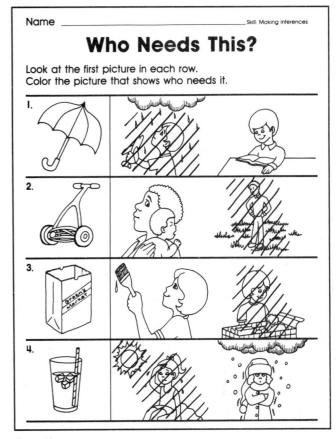

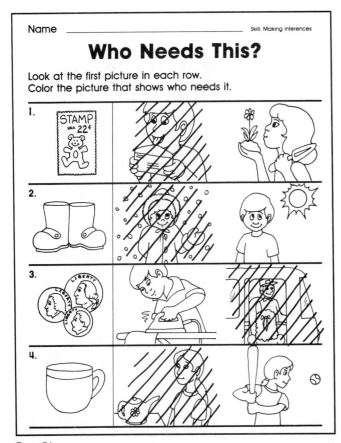

FS-32026 Critical Thinking

Answer Key

Name _____   Skill: Making inferences

Where Are They?

Color the picture that shows where each person is.

Name _____   Skill: Making inferences

What Do They See?

Circle the picture that shows what each one sees.
Color the pictures.

Page 53

Page 54

Name _____   Skill: Making inferences

Time to Pack

Look at the first picture in each row.
Circle the two things you can put in it.

Name _____   Skill: Making inferences

What Can You Make?

Cut and paste to show what you can make.

1. sandwich

2. birdhouse

3. pie

4. mask

Page 55

Page 56

118

FS-32026 Critical Thinking

Answer Key

FS-32026 Critical Thinking

Answer Key

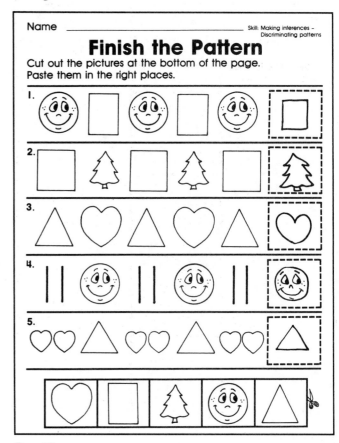

© Frank Schaffer Publications, Inc.

120

FS-32026 Critical Thinking

Answer Key

Name _____
Skill: Making inferences

Where Does It Belong?

Draw a line to show where each thing belongs.
Color the pictures.

Page 65

Name _____
Skill: Making inferences

What Do They Need?

Draw a line to show what each person needs.
Color the pictures.

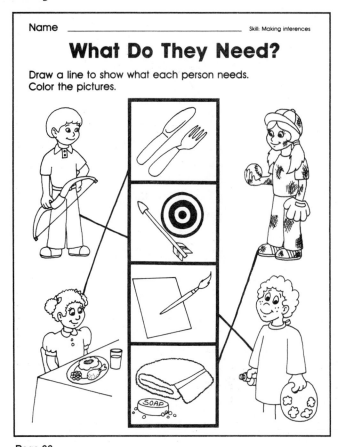

Page 66

Name _____
Skill: Making inferences

Wash Time

Draw a line to show what each person is going to wash.
Color the pictures.

Page 67

Name _____
Skill: Making inferences

Find the Mistakes

Circle the part in each picture that does not belong.
Color all the pictures.

Page 68

FS-32026 Critical Thinking

Answer Key

Name _____

Skill: Making inferences

Find the Mistakes

Circle the part in each picture that does not belong.
Color all the pictures.

Page 69

Name _____

Circle the mistakes.
(There are at least 15.)
Then color the picture.

Page 70

Name _____

Circle the mistakes.
(There are at least 15.)
Then color all the pictures.

Page 71

Name _____

Circle the mistakes in this picture.
(There are at least 22.)
Color the picture.

Page 72

122

FS-32026 Critical Thinking

Answer Key

Page 73

Page 74

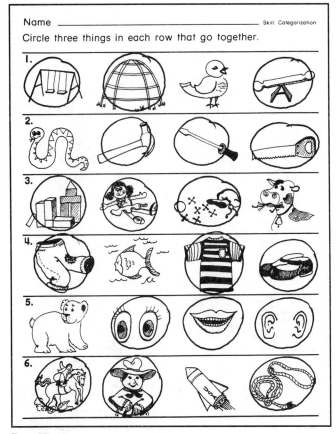

Page 75

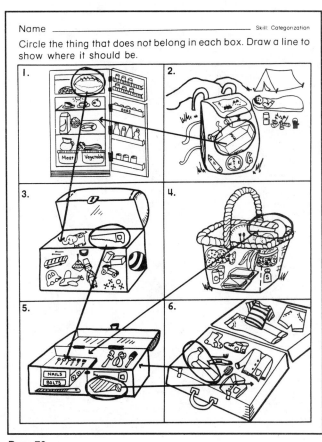

Page 76

Answer Key

Page 77

Page 78

Page 79

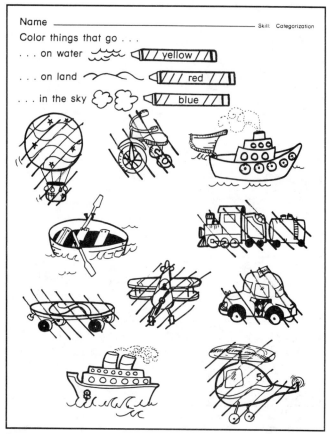

Page 80

124

FS-32026 Critical Thinking

Answer Key

Name ___

Skill: Classification

2. fawn
3. cub
4. lamb
5. foal
6. duckling

calf

Cut out the baby animals below. Paste each baby under its mother.

Page 83

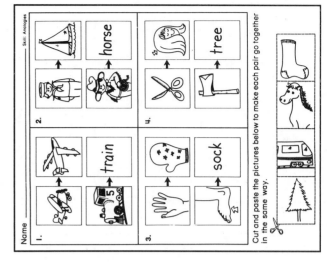

Name ___

Skill: Analogies

1. train
2. horse
3. sock
4. tree

Cut and paste the pictures below to make each pair go together in the same way.

Page 86

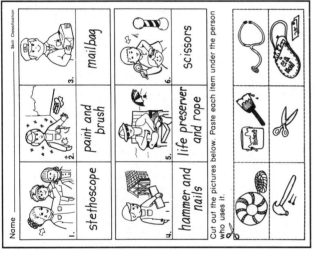

Name ___

Skill: Classification

1. stethoscope
2. paint and brush
3. mailbag
4. hammer and nails
5. life preserver and rope
6. scissors

Cut out the pictures below. Paste each item under the person who uses it.

Page 82

Name ___

Skill: Analogies

1. bed
2. hay
3. tracks
4. Summer clothes

Cut and paste the pictures below to make each pair go together in the same way.

Page 85

Name ___

Skill: Classification

1. target
2. basketball hoop
3. football
4. boxing gloves
5. baseball and baseball glove
6. tennis racket and ball

Cut out the pictures below. Paste each sports item under the person who uses it.

Page 81

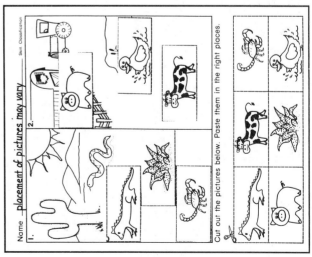

Name _Placement of pictures may vary._

Skill: Classification

1.
2.

Cut out the pictures below. Paste them in the right places.

Page 84

125

Answer Key

Name _____

Find the Causes

Cut and paste the cause to match the effect.

Cause | **Effect** | **Cause**

girl buying peanuts

boy making bed

girl climbing tree

clown waving

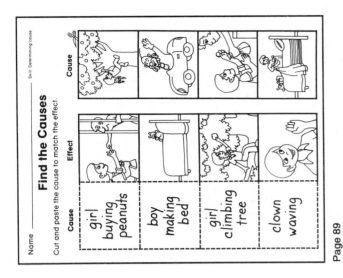

Name _____

Find the Effects

Cut and paste the effect to match the cause.

Effect | **Effect**

broken wishbone

boy ice skating

boy sleeping

blown-out birthday candles

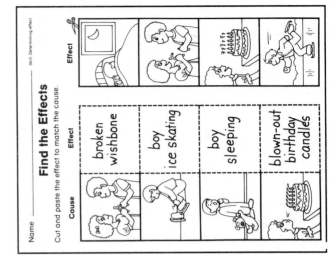

Name _____

Find the Causes

Cut and paste the cause to match the effect.

Effect | **Cause**

rain beginning to fall on picnic

crowing rooster

person feeding fish

kite string breaking

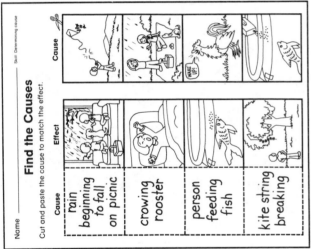

Name _____

Find the Causes

Cut and paste the cause to match the effect.

Cause | **Effect** | **Cause**

spider beginning to spin web

bird sitting in nest

boy rolling bowling ball

people eating a meal

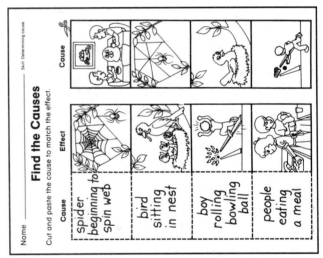

Name _____

1.

ski slope

2.

eggs

screwdriver

3.

4.

speedboat

Cut and paste the pictures below to make each pair go together in the same way.

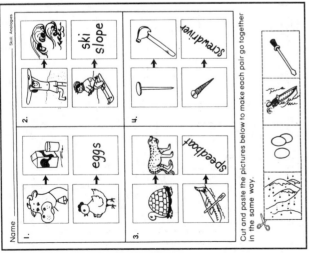

Name _____

Find the Causes

Cut and paste the cause to match the effect.

Cause | **Effect** | **Cause**

thunderstorm

vacuum cleaner

boy bringing rabbit a carrot

girl borrowing library book

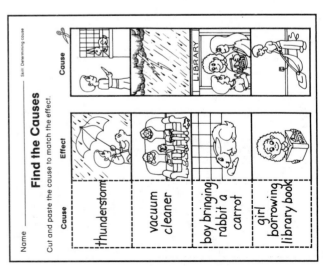

126

FS-32026 Critical Thinking

Answer Key

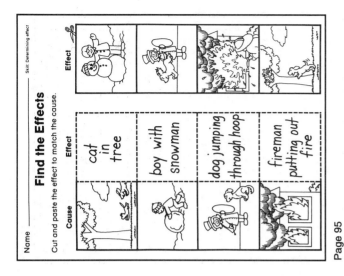

Page 95

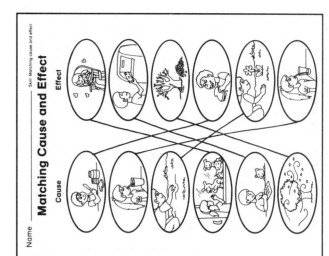

Page 98

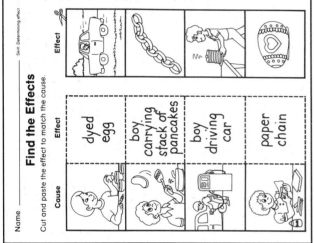

Page 94

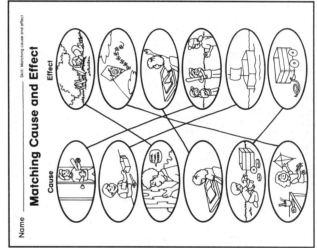

Page 97

Page 93

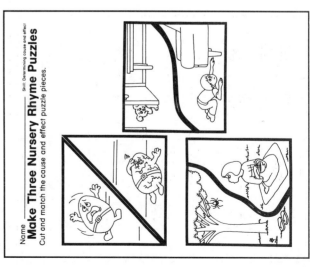

Page 96

Answer Key

Name _____

Skill: Determining multiple causes

What Happened to Make the Flower Grow?
Color the causes of the flower growing.

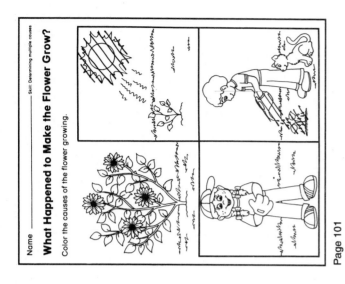

Page 101

Name _____

Skill: Determining multiple effects

What Happens When You Move?

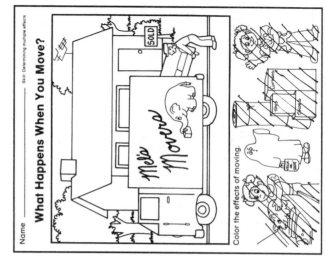

Color the effects of moving.

Page 104

Name _____

Skill: Matching cause and effect

Matching Cause and Effect

Cause   Effect

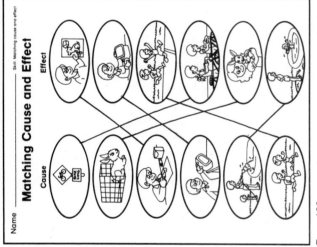

Page 100

Name _____

Skill: Determining multiple effects

What Happens When It Rains?

Color the effects of rain.

Page 103

Name _____

Skill: Matching cause and effect

Matching Cause and Effect

Cause   Effect

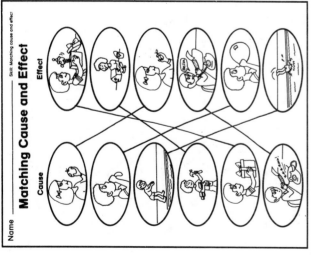

Page 99

Name _____

Skill: Determining multiple causes

What Happened to Make the Rainbow Appear?
Color the causes of the rainbow appearing.

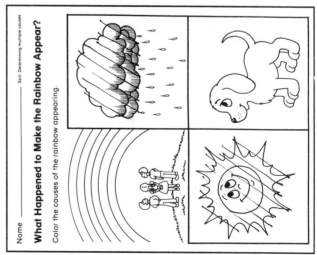

Page 102

128

FS-32026 Critical Thinking